Light Through
The Darkness

When darkness surrounds,

there is light that still shines through.

To my reader,

These are not just poems. They are survival songs. Love letters to the brokenhearted. Whispered prayers when words failed. Cries in the night when no one was listening — or so we thought.
If you're holding this book, maybe you've known the weight of invisible sorrow. Maybe you've begged God for an answer that didn't come the way you hoped. Maybe you've sat in church surrounded by people and still felt completely alone.
This book is for you.
It's for the soul that struggles to speak their pain aloud. For the one who smiles in public and falls apart in private. For the one who believes in God — but still wrestles with doubt, heartbreak, and silence.
These pages don't offer perfect solutions.
What they offer is understanding.
A companion in the valley.
A light in the storm.
And a reminder that just because you've been through the fire doesn't mean you're burned up. It means you're refined.
So read these poems slowly. Let them sit with you in the quiet.
And if all you do is breathe while you read — that's enough.
You are seen. You are loved. You are not alone.

—Makenzie Rae

To the ones who never stopped looking for the light,
even when the darkness made it hard to see.

Sometimes, light pierces the darkness in blazing rays.
Other times, it seeps in — soft and slow — one sliver at a time.

Light Through the Darkness

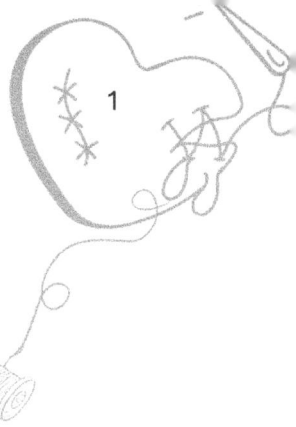

Eyes to See

When the light breaks through,
Even the shadows testify.

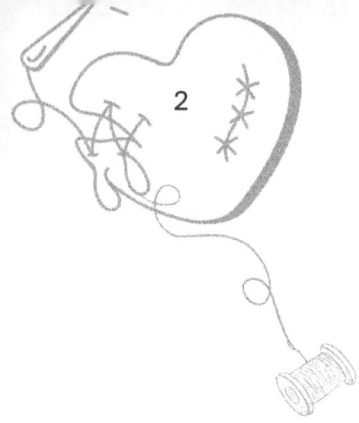

EYES TO SEE

My Prayer

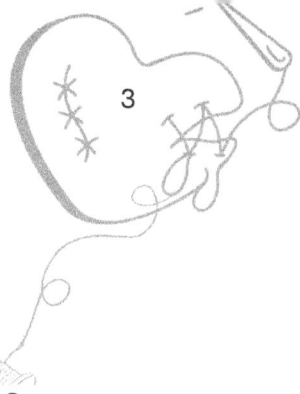

How long do I wait, o Lord?
How long must I live in this valley?
Come and carry me up the mountainside.
Take me in Your arms and deliver me from this heartache.
Lift me out of the despair that has become my life.
I trust in You and know that Your ways are higher than mine.
Bring me to that higher place where pain and suffering are no more.
Move in my life, o Lord.
My joy is in You.
Help me through my sorrow to live in Your joy.
You are my rock and my strength.
Deliver me from the confusion that tries to destroy me.

For You

You may not know me, but truly I know you.
For I have been watching your entire lifetime
through.

I saw you through your trials when life seemed
too hard to bear.
I walked with you in every step, simply because
I care.

You see, I walked on this earth, way before
your time,
To die a criminal's death, though I did not
commit a crime.

On a wooden cross I was crucified.
It was for your sins that I hung and died.

So that now you have forgiveness and a way
back to me,
Just open your heart, let me in, and simply
believe.

Believe that I AM, and what My Word says is
true,
And live for Me every day, in all you say and do.

EYES TO SEE

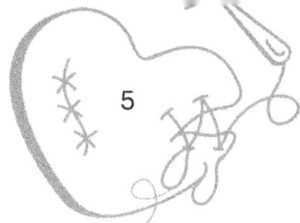

And know that when the battles come, I will see you through.
For I have already won every battle when I was nailed to the cross for you.

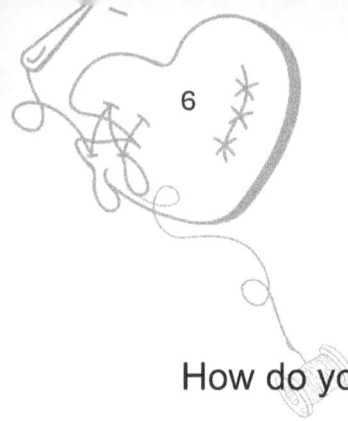

How

How do you know where to go when you cannot
see the way?
How do you choose a direction when your world
is spinning?
How do you climb the mountain when you can't
even move your feet?

How do you hear the voice of God when the
screams of this world fill your ears?
How do you see the will of God when you can't
see past the hardships of life?
How do you reach out in faith when you don't
even have the strength to stand?

How do you keep the faith when it feels like
your world is crashing in?
How do you cry out to God when it seems like
your tears are all dried up?
How do you live for God when living is harder
than breathing?

Sometimes life is hard.
Sometimes you want to give up.
Sometimes it takes all of your energy just to
make it to the next second.

Hold on to Jesus

EYES TO SEE

and He will give you strength.
Keep your eyes on Him
and you will see His will.
Seek after God
and He will lead the way.

Psalm 73:26
My flesh and my heart fail;
But God is the strength of my heart and my
portion forever.

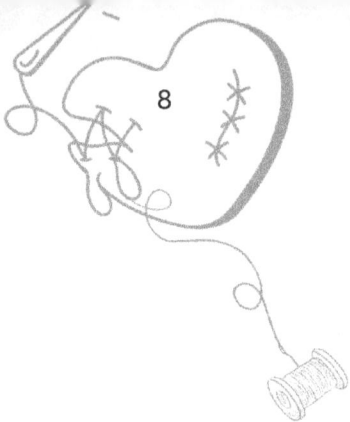

8

EYES TO SEE

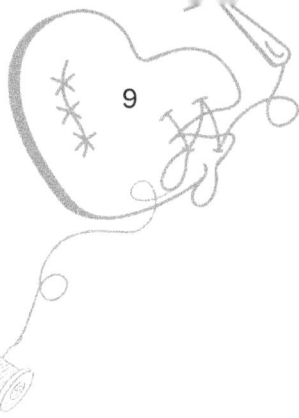

Through the Battles

I sat down to think about
What family really means,
And after much consideration
This is what it is to me.

Family is helping through all of the battles
No matter how short or long.
Family is supporting one another
Even when you know they're wrong.

Family is forgiving
No matter how deep the scar.
Family is helping you stand
When it seems your victory's too far.

Family is always being there
Through the best and worst of days.
Family is us
Today, tomorrow, and always.

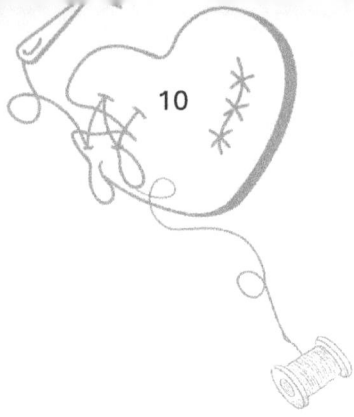

EYES TO SEE

My Mom

I normally hold my feelings in,
But whenever I let them out you are there to
comfort me.

Any time I need to cry,
You are there with a shoulder for me.

When I don't understand about something,
You are there with an answer for me.

You've been there for me all my life,
When I was a child, you raised and taught me.

Well, mom, I'm going to say something straight
from my heart.
Even if I was offered all the money in the world,
I wouldn't give you up as my mom,
My mentor,
And my best friend.

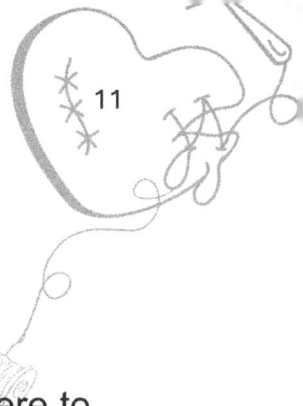

EYES TO SEE

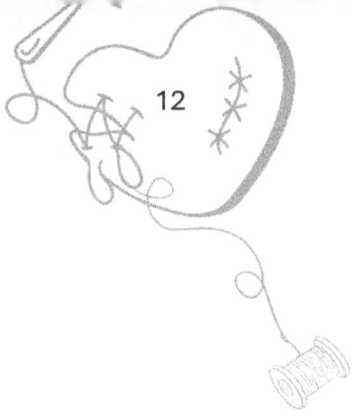

EYES TO SEE

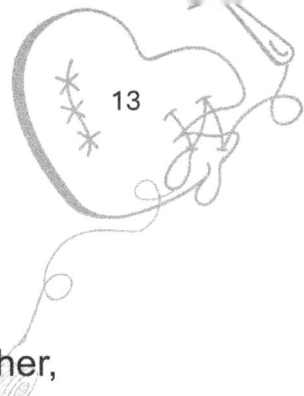

My Brother

I know we don't always work together,
And over the years, between us there's been
some bad weather.

But times have changes and the love grew
stronger,
Now nothing could ever make me love you no
longer.

We may still argue from day to day,
But when people ask me who you are,
"He's my brother," I'm proud to say.

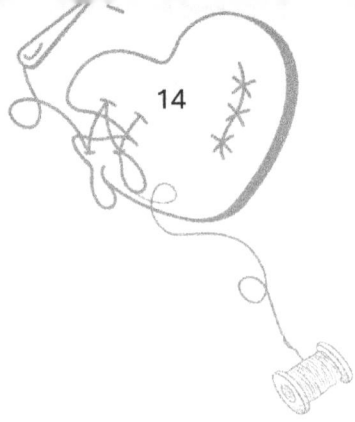

EYES TO SEE

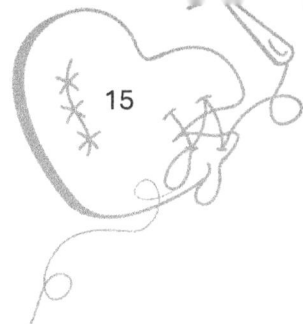

My Friend

There are times throughout our lives
When trials and tribulations come our way,
And the worries of this life seem so heavy
That we fear we won't make it another day.

It's times like these we look to find
Someone who will be there to hold our hand,
Who will listen to us vent our woes,
Someone who will understand.

We need someone to tell us
That everything will be alright,
Who will sit with us and pray with us
Through what can seem an endless night.

A friend is always there
Through the best and the worst of times,
So every day I say a prayer
Thanking God that you are mine.

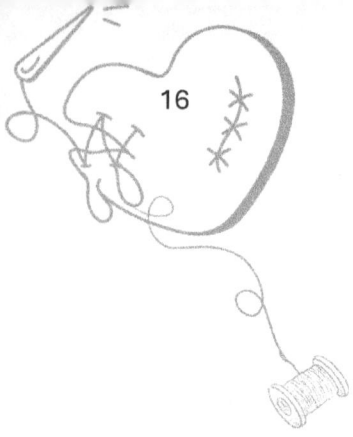

EYES TO SEE

My Home

Please can you help me,
I'm looking for my home.
I know it used to be here,
but now it seems it's gone.

I've searched far and wide,
and it seems to no avail.
Why my home has disappeared
I may never tell.

I very much enjoyed
this home in which I lived,
I tried hard to keep it nice,
everything to it I did give.

A lifetime of love
is what I had to share,
I cared for it and nurtured it;
its walls were never bare.

You see, I was very picky
on all that I did use,
The walls were made of olive wood;
it was the only one I would choose.

Then I painted the walls a beautiful red,
applying just the right amount,
To cover the many blemishes
of which one could not count.

EYES TO SEE

I even added a sunroof
to let the sun shine in,
It shone through the entire house,
around every curve and bend.

And throughout the time I stayed there,
I tweaked and I pruned,
To make my home amazing;
it was wonderful to view.

But it seems to have disappeared
right into thin air,
I can still see the structure
but now its walls are bare.

I would really like to find it
and come back home to stay,
Please can anyone help me
to try and find my way?

I'm sure it can't be far,
for I was there just yesterday,
Things couldn't change so much
from one evening to one day.

I will not give up this search,
my home again I'll find,
For I will seek without ceasing,
lest I run out of time.

EYES TO SEE

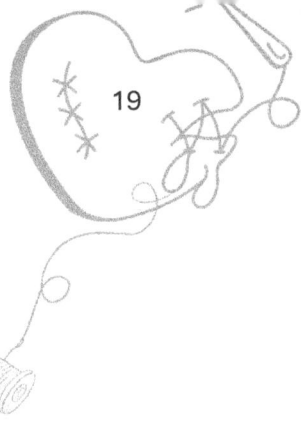

For there is one out there
who is trying to steal my land,
He makes his offers look nice,
lending a seemingly good hand.

He paints beautiful pictures,
saying that red is not enough,
That the house needs more colors,
and to be filled with other stuff.

Stuff that will kill my home
by drowning out its light,
So instead of seeing sunshine,
it would see only night.

I will continue searching,
for my home I know I'll find,
But for a little help
I'll ask you one more time.

Please can you help me,
I am looking for my home,
I know it used to be here,
but now it seems it's gone.

EYES TO SEE

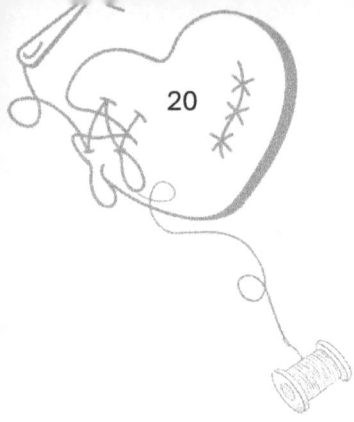

EYES TO SEE

Nature

I open my mouth to tell of Your greatness
But the words I start to utter fall short
They do not do justice in describing Your
awesomeness
I yearn to know how to bless You
I close my eyes and listen to the praises that
surround me
I hear the birds call out Your glory
The trees wave their branches in worship
The water flows in its desire to reach You
I feel the breeze of Your spirit brush my cheek
It caresses my hair and surrounds me
Lord, just as Yours does, let my very nature
give praise and honor to You

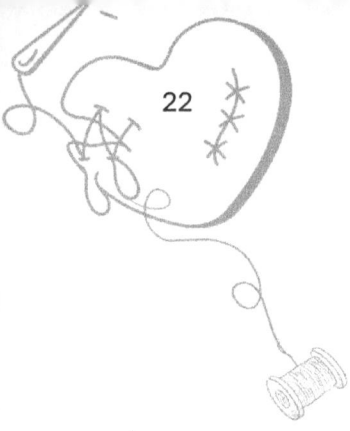

22

EYES TO SEE

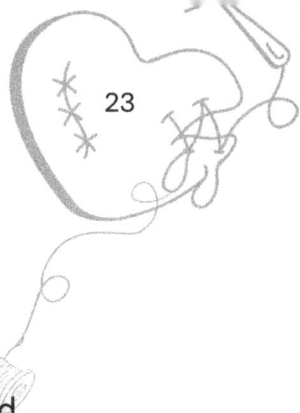

Snowflakes

I look outside my window
And see the snowflakes all around,
Floating gracefully through the air
And landing peacefully on the ground.

I know each one is special
For no two are the same,
It's then I am reminded
That this is how we were made.

Lovingly and tenderly
God made us each unique,
In the actions that we take
And the ways in which we speak.

So the next time that you meet someone
Who seems completely different from you,
It's then I want you to remember
The snowflakes are different too.

Guidance

I have traveled down this road of faith for quite
a bit of time,
With its rights and wrongs and do's and don'ts
that told me, "You must walk this line."

But somewhere along this road I was met with a
choice.
One that allowed me to be free and one that
stole my voice.

If I choose the one that sets me free, I shall
surely be cast out,
But if I choose the one that steals my voice, my
seeds of faith may never sprout.

I must now make a decision that will forever
change my life,
I only want to choose the one that will bring me
closer to Christ.

I have my convictions, and I have my faith,
But since they aren't the same as others', I
need God to show me the way.

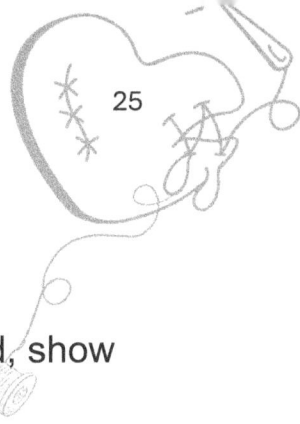

At this crossroad in my road of life, Lord, show
me which way to go.
I can't walk without Your guidance, Jesus, I
really need to know.

Please tell me the direction that You would have
me take.
Let Your hand be with me and help me not to
make a mistake.

I love You, Lord, with all my heart and I believe
that I shall see
That whatever choice I make in life, You will
never leave nor forsake me.

So I pray Your name over my every choice,
And now I will be still, so that I can hear Your
voice.

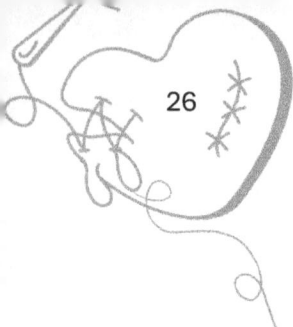

The Dream I Forgot

When I was a child, I did honestly believe,
That one day my prince charming would come
and rescue me.

Life began to happen with its many twists and
turns,
With problems I had to face and bridges I had
to burn.

So many scars and bruises I got along the way,
I simply stopped believing he would come and
save the day.

Then one day it happened that our two paths
did meet,
And instantly forged together a life so full and
sweet.

I can look into your eyes, so caring, soft and
blue,
And know with all my heart that I want to share
my life with you.

EYES TO SEE

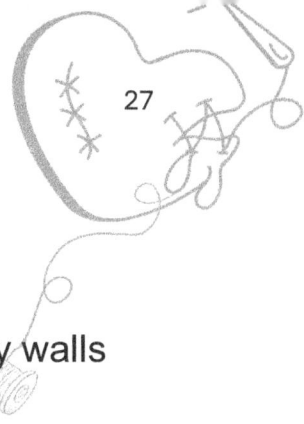

Leaning into your warm embrace my walls
began to melt,
The love that I find there is more than I've ever
felt.

So now I cannot wait to see the rest of my life,
And live the dream that once dreamt as your
companion,
Your friend,
Your wife.

EYES TO SEE

Anchored in Grace

Grace isn't soft –
It's the rope that pulls you up from the deep.

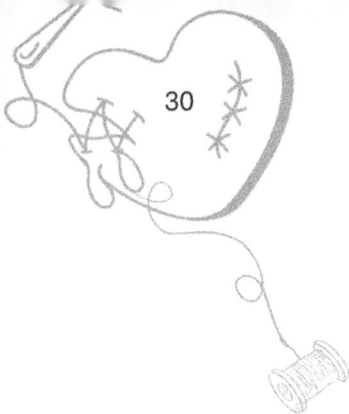

30

ANCHORED IN GRACE

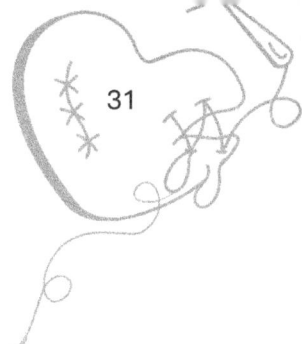

A Prayer

I am searching, but cannot find,
the answers to the questions in my mind.

I feel like I am sinking further and further each
day,
with so many barriers that are blocking my way.

Keeping me from reaching You and grasping
Your hand,
from letting You pull me out of this quickly
sinking sand.

I am suffocating in the thick of this storm;
oh, how I long for the answers to form.

Give me direction, Lord, on which way I should
go,
and tell me the answers that I really need to
know.

ANCHORED IN GRACE

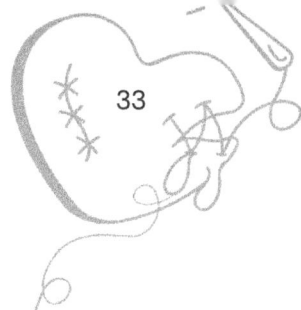

My Garden

I was working in my garden today
Grooming and watering my seeds,
When I saw you, my child
Attempting to prune a tree.

I started to approach
And ask why you were here,
Trying to take my place
In this work I hold so dear.

You see, it is my job and my honor
To care for these plants I love,
To weed them and to bend them
Into what they should become.

I'm truly sorry, my precious child,
But I must ask that you not continue,
For this work I love is never done
And it's time for me to mold you.

I may need to let some of the weeds grow
And may even plant a bush,
For you see, for some of my trees to bend
They need me to give them a little push.

So I am asking you, my child
To let my will be done,
By taking care of all my plants
And molding them with my love.

What Do You See

When you look into my eyes, tell me what you
see.
Do you see the peace and joy radiating from
within me?

Do you see the love I hold deep down inside,
The salvation given me by Christ crucified?

Or do you see the battle, and the struggle that's
within,
To fight back the pain from the scars that were
given?

For many battles I did fight, some seemed too
hard to bear,
I took many painful hits, for the devil does not
fight fair.

He hit me below the belt, hurting those I hold
most dear.
Causing me to carry burdens such as grief and
pain and fear.

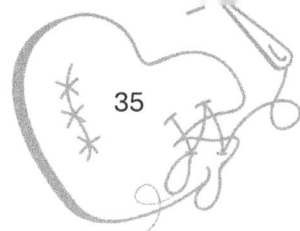

Long and wearily, I walked on intending to win
the fight,
But knew that I could not unless I held on tight.

So tightly I clung to my savior's Word, for I
knew what He said was true,
That no matter how hard the battle, He would
bring me through.

I gave over to Him all the burdens I did keep
And He took me in His arms as I began to
weep.

Such relief I did feel when He wiped away my
pain
He took away my guilt, my sorrow and my
shame.

So even to this day as the war rages on
The devil still attacks, but on Christ's love I
depend upon.

What is it that you see when you look into my
eyes?
I hope you see the love of Christ crucified.

ANCHORED IN GRACE

My Great God

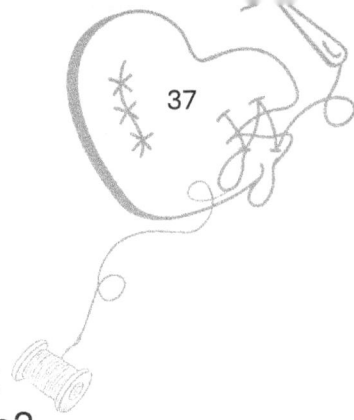

Do you know how great
Is the God in whom I serve?
He gives peace in my storm, joy in my pain,
And grace that I will never deserve.

He never stops loving me
Through the endless, troubling times,
When I'm stumbling through the valleys
Or up the mountains, on my own, I try to climb.

He opens up the window
When all the doors get slammed,
And when my enemies try to destroy me
He sends a host of angels to take command.

He never leaves nor forsakes me
The many times I fail,
And when I think there is no way to win
He gives me the strength to prevail.

I know how great is the God
In whom I trust and believe,
For though I am a sinner and unworthy of it,
His love will never leave.

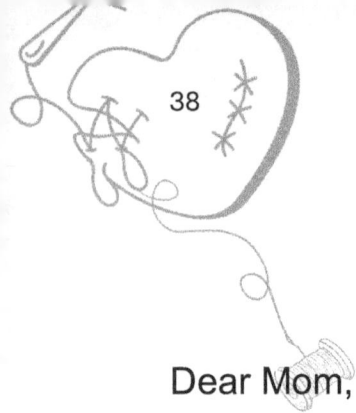

A Poem For My Mom

Dear Mom,

You may not know this, but just before my birth,
I had a talk with God about my life here on
Earth.

I remember very faintly how the conversation
went.
This is what was said just before I was sent.

"Are you sure you want to go and leave this
Heavenly place?"
"Yes, Lord, more than anything I want to see my
mother's face."

"You know she isn't perfect, and you will not
have everything you've dreamed."
"Yes, I know I won't have everything, but I will
get what I need."

"One more question, before it's time for you to
go.
Why choose her, I would really like to know?"

A Poem For My Mom

Dear Mom,

You may not know this, but just before my birth,
I had a talk with God about my life here on
Earth.

I remember very faintly how the conversation
went.
This is what was said just before I was sent.

"Are you sure you want to go and leave this
Heavenly place?"
"Yes, Lord, more than anything I want to see my
mother's face."

"You know she isn't perfect, and you will not
have everything you've dreamed."
"Yes, I know I won't have everything, but I will
get what I need."

"One more question, before it's time for you to
go.
Why choose her, I would really like to know?"

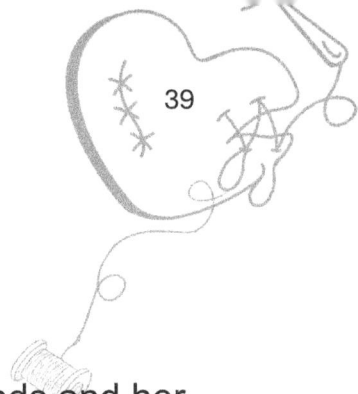

"Because her love will know no bounds and her
faith in me will be
Higher than the mountains and deeper than the
sea.

And although she isn't perfect,
She is perfect
For me."

40

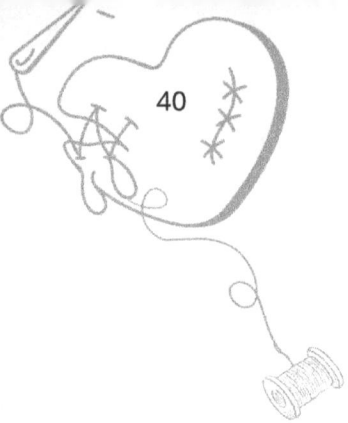

ANCHORED IN GRACE

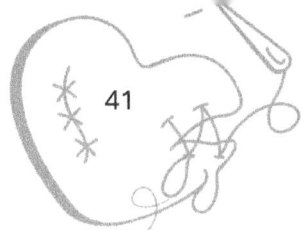

City on a Hill

I see a city set on a hill,
its lights so brightly shine.
I want to find the source of light;
I long to make it mine.

I have lived in this valley,
with its gloom and despair;
The weight of bad decisions
much more than I can bear.

Still on along I trod,
stumbling as I go,
I wish that I could see the face
of the one I used to know.

He used to hold me in His arms
and wash my pain away,
He walked with me and held me close
each and every day.

I remember the peace that I would feel
every time I called His name,
But with all the things that I have done
it will never be the same.

I turned my back and walked away
from the Love I held so dear,
The Love that saw me as I was,
and with whom I had no fear.

I knew He would protect me
and never let me go,
He would pick me up and carry me
when I was feeling low.

I can see the path going up the hill,
the one that leads me back,
But fear alone holds me still,
afraid I'll, once again, go off track.

You see I have climbed this hill before,
back when I was young,
Leaving the world and the wants thereof
was the hardest thing I had ever done.

But standing here at the bottom
having to face this giant again,
Is harder for me now
than it was for me back then.

New regrets and circumstances
now keep me from moving on,
I'm afraid that His love for me
is now and forever gone.

ANCHORED IN GRACE

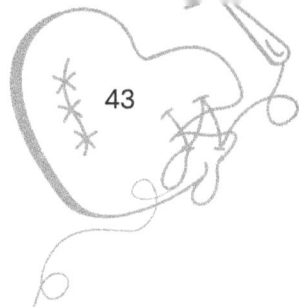

But lo, I see a hand reach down,
and oh, the help it offers me,
It wants to guide me further up;
it wants to make me free.

I will take His hand
and hold on tight.
I will trust in Him
to guide me through the night.

He will lead me past
all the things that I had done,
And through all the storms
that are sure to come.

I am like a city set on a hill
whose light does brightly shine,
I now have found the source of light;
I have once again made it mine.

44

ANCHORED IN GRACE

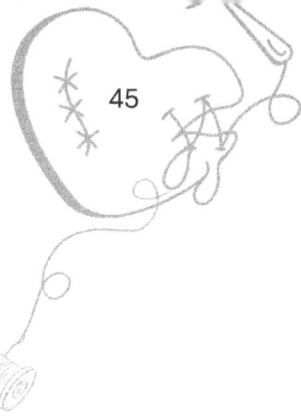

Yours

Opened up and broken, God,
I fully surrender to You,
All the pain, the tears, and the sorrow
Of all the trials I've been through.

Take them all right now,
And let them burden me no more.
I am giving You my life, Lord,
All that I am is Yours.

Forgive me of the sins
That still plague my heavy heart.
Cleanse me of them all, I pray,
And create in me a fresh start.

I ask You, God, to search my soul,
Removing any barriers from within me,
So You can make me, Lord, and mold me
Into what You would have me be.

Or

Why do you love God?

Is it because He stepped off His throne and willingly laid His life down for you?
Or is it because of the blessings that He has in store for you?

Do you seek to know Him and His will better?
Or do you only seek the things you want Him to give you?

If His answer doesn't line up with what you want, will you still follow Him?
Or will you say that God doesn't love you because your prayers weren't answered the way you thought they should be?

Will you be like the three Hebrew boys and say, "But if not, He is still good"?
Or will you decide in your heart that since He didn't, He's not?

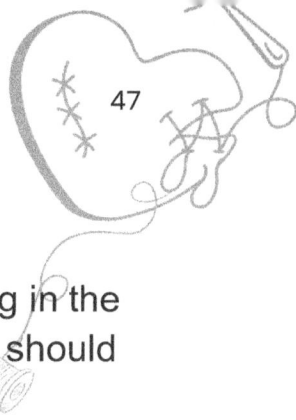

When life's burdens keep you wandering in the
wilderness longer than you thought you should
be, will you be faithful?
Or will you turn to other things, other gods, and
forget the ways God has already blessed you?

Do you love God simply because He is God;
Elohim; Adonai; El Shaddai?
Or because you believe you'll be blessed if you
do?

When the struggles of life get heavy, will you
fold under the weight of them?
Or will you stand firm, knowing that this life is
temporary and a greater one is yet to come?

If asked why you love God, will you state only
the material things that He has given you in this
life?
Or will you proudly proclaim His sacrifice that
will allow you to spend eternity with Him?

Search your soul and determine:
Why do you love God?

My Desire

I long to live for You
Not looking left or right
Walking through the fire
Always keeping You in sight

Obstacles come before me
Trying to obstruct my view
They continually try to stop me
From walking this path to You

I try to go around them
And continue on this course
But I need the true power
From which You are the only source

God, I need You to come
For I feel my faith may fail
The obstacles grow bigger
And make Your light seem pale

I know that if I trust You
You will help to bring me through
But right now, I need this mountain moved
Because it's getting harder to see You

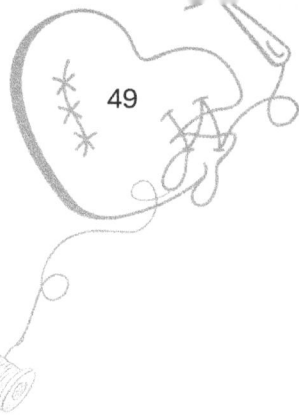

I lift my hands to You
For I honestly believe
That if I keep my eyes on You
I will always receive

Receive the strength I need
To walk on through the flame
And move all the mountains
By praising Your holy name

Thank You, Lord, for the power
And the peace that You give
In the troubled times
Of this life that I live

I know that when I seek You first
Things won't stay the same
So I will keep believing
And trusting in Your name

ANCHORED IN GRACE

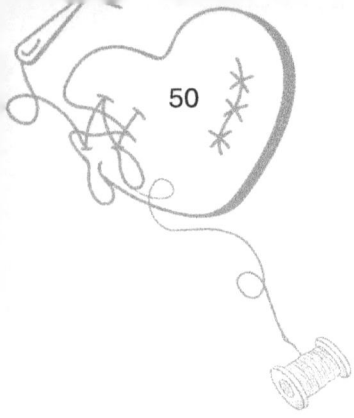

ANCHORED IN GRACE

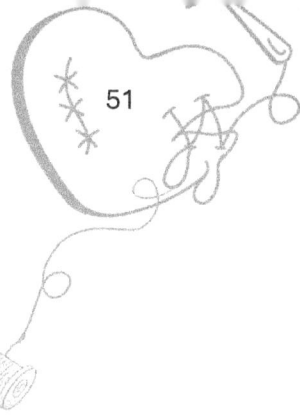

I'm Good

When things are going good in my life
I smile and say I'm good
Why
Because at that moment I'm not struggling with
much
Troubles aren't trying to weigh me down
I'm actually doing good

When things are going bad in my life
I smile and say I'm good
Why
Because at that moment I'm struggling with a
lot of stuff
But I know who fights my battles
Troubles are trying to weigh me down
But I know who lifts me up
I'm not actually doing good
But I know the One who works it together for
my good

I Am

Out beyond the city walls,
Up upon a hill so high,
Out to forgive the sins of man,
Up on the cross, alone, stood I.

I Am the rock that holds you up,
I Am the wind that blows your hair,
I Am the hand that keeps you safe,
I Am the heart that shows you care.

I Am the feet that guide your way,
I Am the eyes that let you see,
I Am the One who loves you deeply,
Here I stand, alone, it's Me.

I Am the joy that makes you happy,
I Am the hope that makes you strong,
I Am the peace that gives you comfort,
I Am the rhythm of your heart's song.

I Am the love that keeps you warm,
I Am the victory that ends all strife,
I Am the arms that hold you close,
I Am the breath that gives you life.

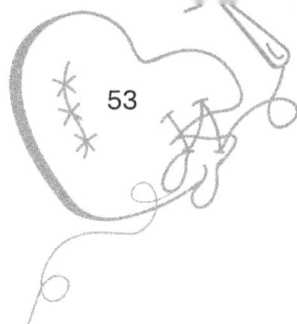

I wait to look into your eyes,
I wait to greet you face to face,
I wait to say how much I love you,
And show you around this Heavenly place.

So when you think you will not make it,
And you feel you can't go on,
Just remember that I love you,
I'm the One who makes your fears be gone.

I'll give you water in your desert,
I'll speak peace to calm your storm,
Just praise your way through every trial,
And don't be afraid to step out of "the norm".

When you feel you're being persecuted,
And you do not understand,
Just lift your eyes to Heaven,
And simply believe that I Am.

Out beyond the blazing valleys,
Out beyond the mountains high,
Out beyond the star swept nights,
There alone, waiting, stands I.

54

ANCHORED IN GRACE

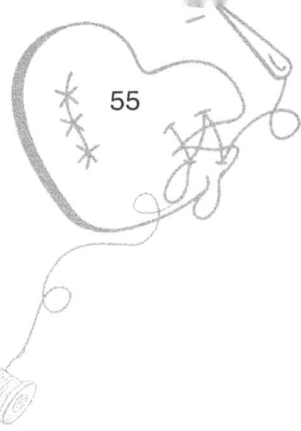

In the Morning

If you wake up in the morning
And you cannot see the light
And it feels as if you're waking
In the dead of night.

It may seem you're all alone
And you cannot find a friend
Keep holding on to faith
For your night is about to end.

Joy comes in the morning
And the darkness will shortly flee
Just keep your eyes on Jesus
And you will begin to see.

He'll help you through your night
And your burdens He will bear
And no matter what the trial
He always will be there.

Me

Write a poem about me they say,
But only talk about the good.
It seems like it should be easy,
Oh, that I wish it would.

I know that I am loving.
I know that I am strong.
I know I'm quick to forgive
For every time that I've been wronged.

I like to make people smile,
To put joy inside their heart
I welcome people into my family
Right from the very start.

I've always got a hand
For anyone in need.
"If it's in my power, I'll help"
Has always been my creed.

But these are just surface level,
The things everyone can see.
Beneath the face I show the world
Is a very deeper me.

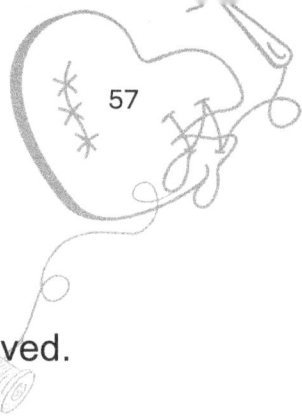

I know that I am loving,
Because I know how it feels to not be loved.
I know that I am strong,
Because I've had to pick myself up after being shoved.

I'm quick to forgive a wrong,
For I was taught that's what you do,
Even if it seems too big a mistake,
Because I've made a wrong or two.

I like to make people smile,
Because I know what it's like to be sad.
I bring joy to people's hearts,
Because it helps make the horrible a little less bad.

I don't make people wait
To be included on the pages of my heart,
Because sometimes it's hard for us to trust,
To believe that we are an important part.

I know I have a hard time
Saying no to anyone who asks.
I never want for them to feel
That they're alone in any task.

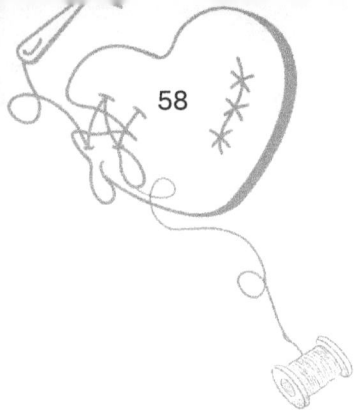

ANCHORED IN GRACE

All of Me

When I think about who I am
I find it hard to explain
I can list my good traits
I'm strong, I'm loving, I'm kind
I genuinely want to see people do great things
It's like I'm listing attributes of a prize pony
Fast, strong, will win any race
I can also tell you my flaws
I'm insecure, I overthink, I'm too independent
I trust too quickly, which leaves me broken
inside
It's like I'm picking out fruit at a grocery store
Too soft, too hard, too many bruises
All of these traits are true about me
But you can't take one without the other
I would be living a lie
To live me, is to live *all* of me
The fun, easy going me and the scared, broken
me
What I am learning about who I am
Is that I am me
All of me
The good, bad, ugly, pretty, scarred, healing,
confident, insecure, growing
Imperfectly perfect me
And that is enough

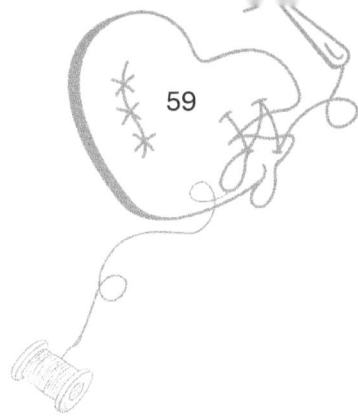

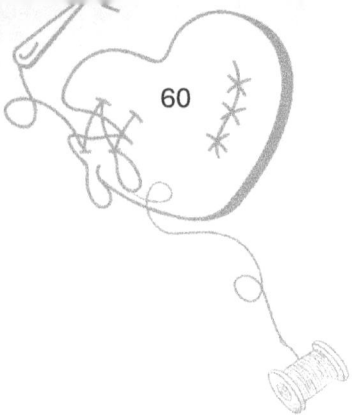

ANCHORED IN GRACE

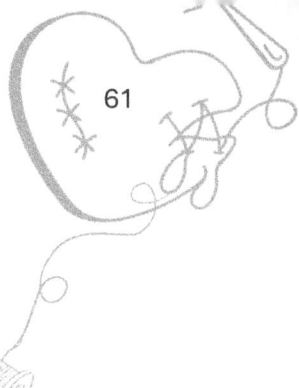

From Ashes to Authority

Out of the cinders came a voice,
Steady and sure –
I am still here.

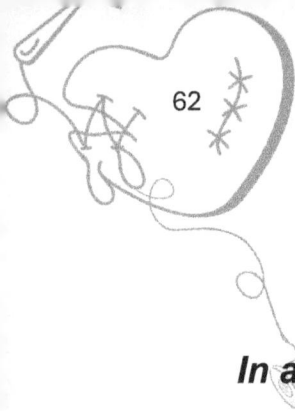

Overcome

Romans 8:37
In all these things, we are MORE than CONQUERORS…

I look to the skies and see the storm clouds
rolling closer in. I will not worry.
I can overcome.

I see the lightning strike the ground and feel its
electricity flow through my body. I will not fear.
I can overcome.

I hear the thunder busting through my
eardrums. I will not be shaken.
I can overcome.

I feel the pellets of rain strike hard against the
flesh on my bones. I will not run.
I can overcome.

I feel the weight of the water trying to drag me
to the ground. I will not stumble.
I can overcome.

I feel the water rising higher trying to drown me
in its pool. I will not sink.
I can overcome.

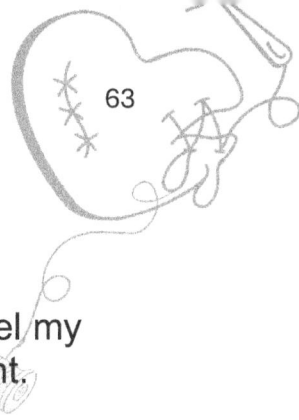

As the storm continues to come, I feel my
energy start to drain. I will not faint.
I can overcome.

I look past the storm and see the clearing skies
ahead. I will hold tight to faith.
I can overcome.

When the devil tries to weigh me down with the
storms of this life, I will not fall.
I can overcome.

Trust in the Lord with all your heart,
And lean not unto your own understanding,
Remember the Lord in all you do,
And He will give you success.
Proverbs 3:5

FROM ASHES TO AUTHORITY

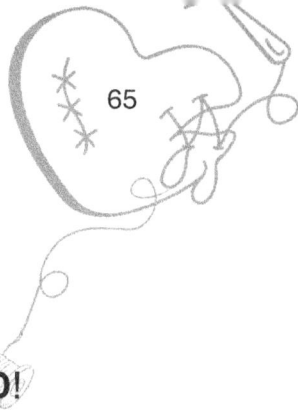

Stand

When life gets you down, **STAND!**

When faith seems small, **BELIEVE!**

When hope runs low, **DREAM!**

When you feel like you are falling, **HOLD TIGHT!**

Sometimes in life we get disappointed with the cards that we were dealt. We feel like we have been pushed away, kicked around, and knocked out. We don't want to go on another day. But if we can learn to **STAND** strong and **BELIEVE** in a **DREAM** and **HOLD TIGHT** with every ounce of energy we have, we will see that the cards we were dealt turned out to be a **ROYAL FLUSH!** We are loved by a **ROYAL** God who came to earth to **FLUSH** our sins and our worries and our pains and our frustrations down the drain. Keep faith and believe that He will see you through every battle.

Love

How do you define love?
How do you give it an explanation?

Do you use big words that have deep meaning?
Do you use small words that have a lot of
emotion?

Love is the moon that smiles down when
everything else is dark.
The stars that light up the night sky.

Love is the brilliant colors of a single rainbow
after a big storm.
The rays of sunshine that escape from behind
the clouds.

Love is the river that carries hope to the desert
lands.
The lake that cools down a hot summer's day.

Love is the tree that provides shelter from the
heat of the sun.
The flower that gives beauty to everything
around it.

Love is laying down in your bed at the end of a
long day.
The faith that you cling to when things are going
bad.

How do I define love?
It's the beat that my heart skips
when I open my phone and see a text from you.

It's the smile on my lips
when I think about you.

It's the twinkle in my eyes
when I am looking into yours.

Love is us,
me and you,
now and forever and always.

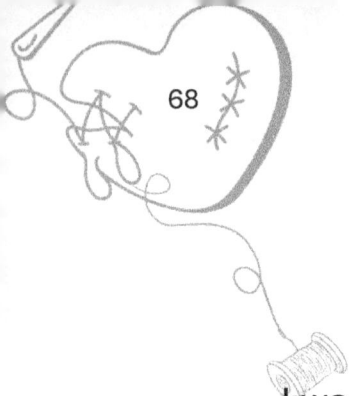

I Know

I was walking down the road of life
when who did I happen to see?
It was Jesus Christ, my Lord and Savior
come to walk a while with me.

"How are you doing today, my child?"
He asked with loving eyes.
"I suppose that I am good,"
Was all I could reply.

Suddenly He stopped
and He turned away His head.
I couldn't help but wonder,
Was it something I'd said?

"Lord, please tell me what is wrong,
and why You turned away."
I saw the sadness in His eyes
when He turned to face my way.

"You say that you are good,
but there is sorrow in your heart.
Tell me, my child,
why did these feelings start?"

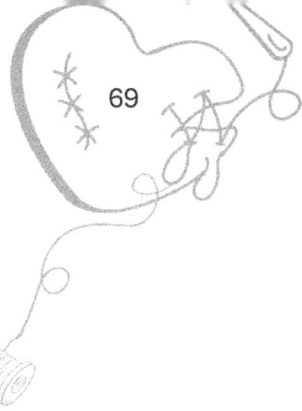

I didn't really know
exactly what I should say.
And as I began to talk,
I turned my head away.

"My baby got sick
and my heart just sank.
All of my bills are due,
but I have no money in the bank.

I prayed for You to fix things
and make everything alright,
And I even read my bible
each and every night.

And still You didn't come
to take away my strife.
I just feel like You don't care
about me or my life.

For if You truly loved me
You would come to rescue me.
But instead, I am drowning
in this great and mighty sea."

I snapped my mouth shut,
I couldn't believe what I had said.
Yes, that is how I felt,
but I usually kept it in my head.

Slowly I looked up
and dared to take a peek,
And sucked in my breath
when I saw the tears fall down His cheek.

"Lord, I'm very sorry.
That's not what I meant to say.
Everything is good;
I'm just having a bad day."

He took a deep breath in,
and held it for a moment,
"It's ok, my child.
I know exactly what you meant.

You see Me now
as a great and mighty God,
But you didn't see me back
when on this earth I did trod.

You see, I was all man,

just the same as you.
And believe me when I say
that I had bad days too.

I had to look into the eyes
of the man who would betray me,
And lead the soldiers to find me
for just a bit of money.

I got beat with a whip,
had stripes on my back,
Climbed up a long hill;
My own cross I had to pack.

The splinters from the wood
dug deep into my wounds,
And it was in that very moment
that I thought of you.

I knew that without my death,
you could not live.
So on the cross I was nailed,
your sins to forgive."

I fell down at His feet
and started to repent,
"You see, my child," He said quietly,
"I know exactly what you meant."

FROM ASHES TO AUTHORITY

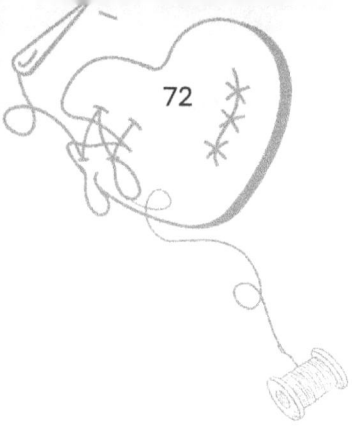

72

FROM ASHES TO AUTHORITY

Endure

They say to run this race with perseverance
But what do you do when you are barely
standing
When it takes every ounce of energy you have
to remain upright
When what you really want to do is lie down
and curl up in a ball
Protect yourself from the arrows that are being
flung at you from all directions
To just surrender to darkness
The freedom and release it offers
The promise of happiness
The assurance of peace
I can't stand alone any longer
So I will sit in the silence and wait
Wait for the Redeemer to come and renew my
strength
To lift me up from my sorrow and bring into His
joy
His peace
No matter how long it takes
I will wait

FROM ASHES TO AUTHORITY

Rejoice

Be thou ready, oh my soul,
For the miracles of God are raining down.
Open your hands and receive
the blessings that were promised you.
Now is the time to believe.
Claim your reward and boast in His power.
The enemy has tried to defeat you,
telling you lies of ugly untruths.
You're worthless.
You're not good enough.
Smart enough.
Brave enough.
Bold enough.
LIES!
You have within you the power to overcome!
For He who lives in you is greater than he who
is in the world.
Than he who whispers in your ear.
God's word has given you the weapon to
destroy the enemy.
It is sharp enough to slice through the barriers
that the enemy tries to place in front of you.
Use it to break free.
Let go of the pains,

the hurts,
the shames of yesterday.
Let God break the power of yesterday that
holds you hostage.
Let Him do a new thing in you.
Let Him change you into a new creation.
With new goals.
New hopes.
New dreams.
Shout for joy, oh my soul
for the Spirit of God has made you whole.
Has removed that old, broken down vessel
inside
and placed within you a brand new, sparkling
white heart.
A heart that beats only for Him.
That has His blood pumping healing power
throughout.
Rest in Jesus, oh my soul,
when sorrow comes your way.
For He knows your past, your present, and your
future.
He has His covering over you.
His banner over you is love.
He loves you with an everlasting love.

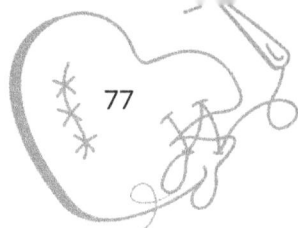

It doesn't end when troubles and sorrows come.
He stands behind you.
Beside you.
And before you.
He encompasses you all around with power to defeat every enemy that comes against you.
Take your place, oh my soul.
Be thou ready to stand.
The time is nigh to do the work of the Lord.
Be thou open to pour out what God has given you.
To shout from the rooftops the greatness of His love.
Don't miss this blessed opportunity to share the good news.
Now is the time to rejoice, oh my soul.
Again, I say it to you,
Rejoice!

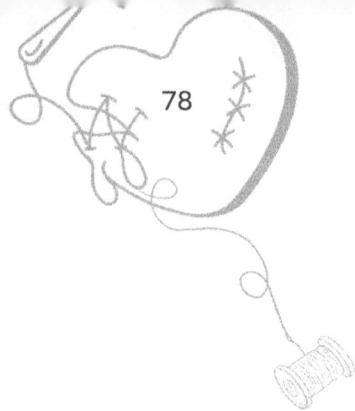

FROM ASHES TO AUTHORITY

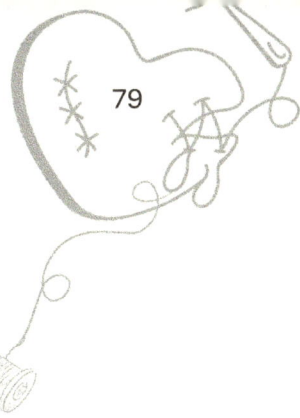

Victory

The joy of the Lord is my hiding place
The freedom I find in His saving grace
Where I met my Savior face to face

I rejoice in the beauty of His endless love
As His Shekinah Glory comes down from above
I see the wonders of all He has done

I rest in Him when I'm feeling weak
He takes me over the mountain's peak
He's always there when His face I seek

He knows my sorrows, and He knows my pain
He gives the clarity that keeps me sane
His love for me will never wane

Over mountains high or valleys low
When the enemy tries to steal my glow
My Savior delivers the winning blow

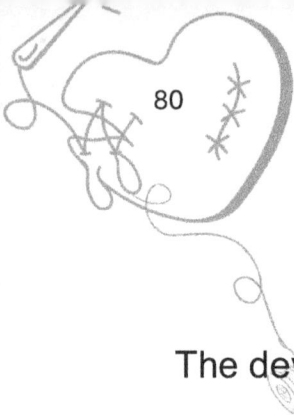

Look Out Devil

The devil is like a roaring lion, roaming to and
fro,
Attacking saints of young and old, so it's time
for us to know.
The devil is not as strong as he wants us to
believe,
His only real power is to lie and deceive,
Us into thinking that we ain't washed in the
blood,
That our sins weren't forgiven by God's sacrifice
of love.
"You ain't good enough, and you never will be,
So why not just surrender your life to me."
That's what the devil whispers in our ears every
night and day,
But saints of God, I challenge you to face the
devil and say,
"The Lord is my light and my salvation, I will *not*
be afraid,
For Jesus' blood has covered me, and my debt
to you *has* been paid.
Way back on Calvary's hill, on an old, rugged
cross,
My God stepped off His throne, so that *I* would
not be lost.
So say what you want now devil, and try to
steal my peace,

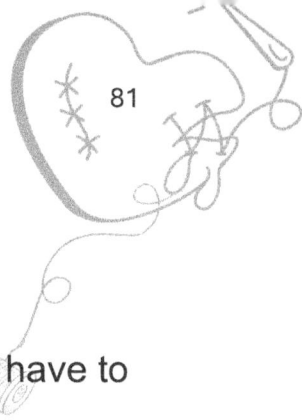

But when I speak in *His* name, you will have to release
Your grip on the minds of my brother and my sister.
And beware devil, because just in case you missed her,
The bride of Christ, *the church of the one and only living God*, is now on the attack.
She is marching over to *your* land, and she is going to take back,
All the souls you stole from her, when she was feeling weak,
See now her strength is up, and it is nearing its peak.
She *will* get her family back, and when *that* battle is through,
Look out devil, 'cause she's comin' after you."

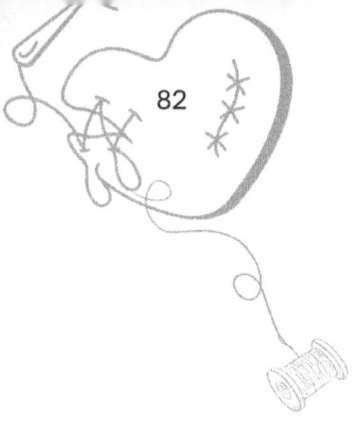

FROM ASHES TO AUTHORITY

Never Give Up

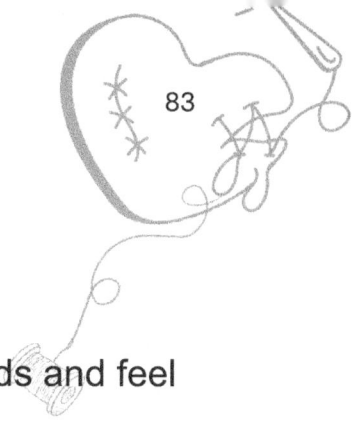

I sit among these majestic wildwoods and feel
so small and inadequate.

They are so tall and strong and bold, while I am
frail and small.

"You, too, will become like us after many more
seasons have passed."

But I am not the young sprouts that are all
around.

I have seen many seasons already but still
must look up to see those that surround me.

They reach up and can touch the sun. They
press down and reach the river that flows deep
below.

I only hear stories about the sun as it is blocked
from me under their never-ending canopies.

I fear I will never know the exhilarating joy of
spreading my arms wide over everyone else.

"Do not give up. You may feel small, but you have grown stronger than you were," I hear.

But I do not feel stronger. I feel like the same little seedling still trying to break through my shell.

I still feel the overwhelming pressure of the seemingly miles and miles of dirt I had to crawl through just to get a breath of air.

I still feel the drowning weight of the floods that rained down on me, often causing me to fall over.

No, I do not feel stronger. I do not feel like I will ever be worthy enough to be among the masses.

I do not know how to be strong enough or brave enough to make myself be seen.

What I do know is that despite the many hardships of my beginnings, I will never stop trying to grow.

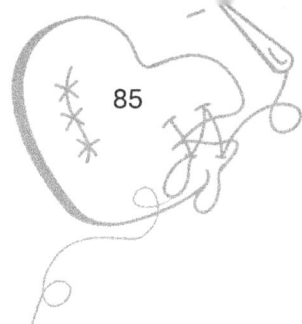

I will use my past as a remembrance of the strength that is buried deep within the heart of me, even when I cannot see it.

I will remember that if I was strong enough to burst out of my shell and crawl through the endless dirt, then I am strong enough to keep trying.

I will keep trying to be strong.
I will keep trying to be bold.
I will keep trying…period.

FROM ASHES TO AUTHORITY

Don't Quit

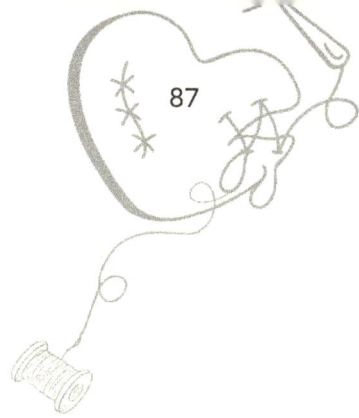

Run
Don't give up
Jog
If you must slowdown
Walk
When it feels you can't continue
Crawl
If your legs get too weak to stand on

Just don't give up!
Don't quit when it gets too hard.
Keep fighting with every drop of energy you
have within you.
Your goal is near, but only if you don't quit.

If life hits you below the belt
Crawl until you catch your breath
When you are able to stand again
Walk while you grow your strength
After you've gained some stamina
Jog along the path you've been set on
Don't look back and don't give up
Run like your life depends on it

Fight Back

How long will we let the devil hurt us?
Steal from us?
Lie to us?
We need to put our foot down and tell him,
"**Enough is enough.**"
If we trust in Jesus and follow His word,
He will fight for us.
He will become the force behind our attack.
Beside our attack.
And in front of our attack.
He will go before us and devour our enemies,
If we let Him.
We need to stop letting the enemy steal this
truth from us.
We need to strike back.
Today is the day for a revolution,
The day for God's people to send up a war cry.

It's time for us to attack.
For us to fight back and quit hiding.
How do we do that?
We use everything we have.
If He has given you the gift of creativity,
Show the beauty from the ashes.
If He has given you the spirit of praise,
Rejoice with your entire being.

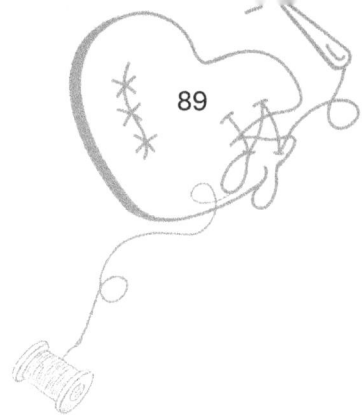

If He put a song in your heart,
Shout out His praises.
HALLELUJAH!
If He has given you the breath of life,
Live everyday giving thanks.
And when you have nothing left inside to fight with,
Cry out to the only One who can do the fighting for you.
JESUS!
He has already paid the price for our victory.
He has already said that we can win,
That we will win!
All we have to do is fight back against the enemy's lies.

"You're not good enough."
"You'll never be good enough."
"You should just quit."
"It's too hard, you should walk away."
"You're not pure enough. Clean enough. Holy enough… You're just not… enough."
"How could Jesus love you? He knows what you've done. What you've said. What you've thought."
"He could never love someone as dirty as you."
"You're nothing but a lying, cheating, worthless human being."
"You are nothing."

LIAR!

Fight back using the enemy's own words.
Stop hiding the hurt, the pain, the ugliness of
the past.
Instead, use it as a declaration.
"I'm not good enough,
But Jesus."
"It is hard,
But Jesus."
"I've done some stuff,
But Jesus."
"I have sinned,
But Jesus."
"I wasn't enough,
BUT JESUS!"

Call out the enemy when he attacks.
"Devil, I know that you want my soul,
But I also know of a God who is stronger than
you.
Smarter than you.
Bigger than you.
Better than you.
You may attack me, beat me up a little, and
maybe even knock me down,
But you should be warned,
I don't fight alone.
The same God that took the keys from you,
Is the same God that lives inside of me.

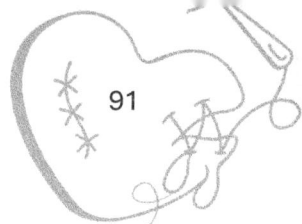

The same God that trampled you under His foot,
Is the same God that stands by my side.
The same God that knocked you out before,
Is the same God that goes before me now.
And you can fight as hard as you want against me,
But my God will defeat you again.
And just when you think you've won,
Beware, because then it's my turn.
I will come against you to take back everything you've stolen from me.
My joy.
My peace.
My happiness.
My song.
My family.
And before you get too confident thinking that I will be defeated,
That I will run and hide,
Just remember,
I don't fight alone."

FROM ASHES TO AUTHORITY

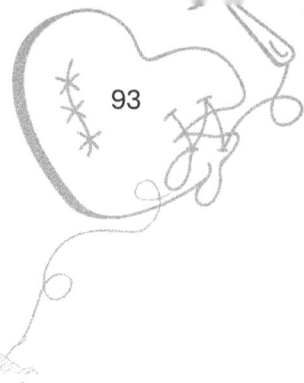

The Light

Cling to the light that is today
For tomorrow's darkness will soon be here
Stealing the vestiges of life you have left
Use the last of your energy to fight back
Battle diligently against the night
Refusing to let it lay waste to your light
Seize every opportunity to live in the now
As death's footsteps lurk nearby
Waiting for the opportunity to spirit you away
Alas, it is inevitable that you will meet him
But until your time has come to completion
Revel in the light that is today

Does the Devil Know Your Name

Darkness draws ever near
As you try to hold your light steady.
It wants to defeat and destroy you,
Let's just pray you're ready.

Your hands start to tremble
And your knees start to knock.
You want to run away
Instead, you stand in shock.

As the darkness starts to surround you,
You remember something from the past,
The lesson you heard on Wednesday night,
Or were you really paying attention in that
class?

You think it is hard to remember just what you
heard,
When suddenly the thought comes.
It was something about calling on Jesus' name
And the devil will be gone.

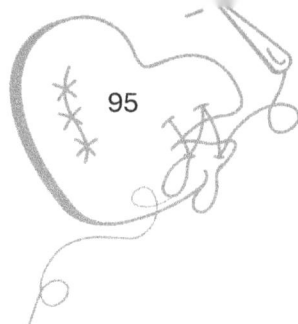

You whisper to the evil that's all around,
"In Jesus name I command you leave."
Now you're safe and don't have to worry,
At least that's what you want to believe.

You try to walk on past the darkness,
But you can't seem to get through,
When you hear a voice saying,
"Jesus and Paul I know, but who are you?"

Are you a sold-out believer
Who does everything they can
To help reach the lost
And save the souls of man?

Does the devil know that when he plays with
you
He will surely lose this game?
Or let me pose another question,

DOES THE DEVIL KNOW *YOUR* NAME?

Brother's Keeper

Shhh.
Quiet.
Be still.
Can you hear it?
Lay down and put your ear to the ground.
Do you hear it now?
What are you supposed to be listening for?
Something that has been trampled beneath the
ever-flowing waves of compromise.
It's the sound that has been buried for far too
long.
The sound that has been extinguished by the
promise of change.
The sound that has been muted by the lies of
progress.
But what exactly is the sound?
It is the voices of our brothers' and sisters'
blood crying up from the ground.
The blood that was stolen by an enemy cloaked
in sheep's clothing.
The blood that continuously saturates the
ground on which we stand.
The blood that we deny.
How long will we sit silently by and let it
happen?
How long will we close our eyes and ears to the
truths that continue to plague our brothers and
sisters?

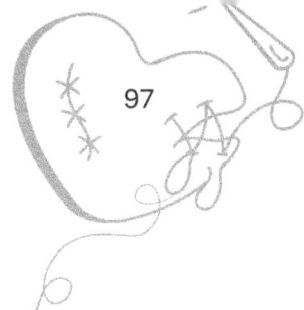

Are we not all one people?
Do we not all bleed the same?
Why do we stand idly by while our families are
being destroyed?
When will we take a stand?
Stand against the hatred that has a controlling
grip on the hearts and minds of far too many
people?
Stand against the injustices that befall our
children and our children's children?
Stand against the lie that stereotyping and
racism isn't still an issue in today's world?
When will we say enough is enough?
When will we stand united with all people, in
love, and demand change?
We must cry out for those whose voices are
silenced by fear.
We must stand for those who are pushed down
and trampled on.
We must break the confines for those who dare
not defy the boundaries that have been placed
on them.
We must be strong for the weak.
We must lift up those who are broken and
hurting.
We must bring love to those who have never
experienced unconditional love.
We must be our brother's keeper.

Seasons

Outside the windows
the snow shines bright,
Reflecting from the sky
the moon's silent light.

The trees are all bare
for their leaves have all gone,
And will not return
until winter is done.

Though they are bare
and seem to be dead,
The trees are not dying
but growing instead.

For without losing its leaves
it would not be able to grow,
So instead of cursing
it welcomes the snow.

Although this rhyme is short
and simple as it may be,
Keep looking deeper
and this truth do see.

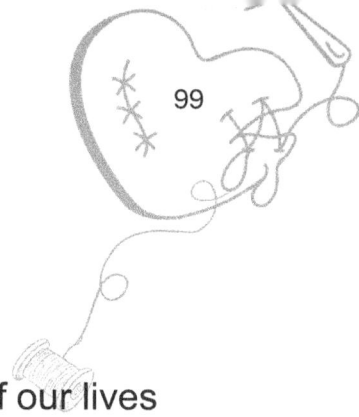

Without change in the seasons of our lives
and if we never lose anything,
We would never grow in our faith
And probably stop believing.

So hold on to God
In the winter of your life,
And He'll bring you through
all your pain and all your strife.

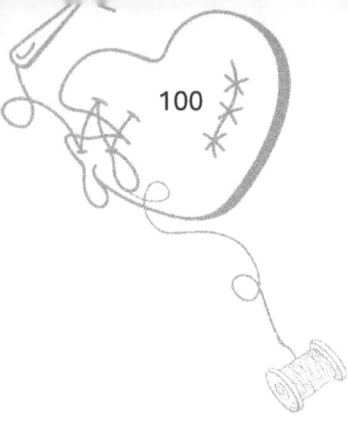

LIGHT THROUGH THE DARKNESS

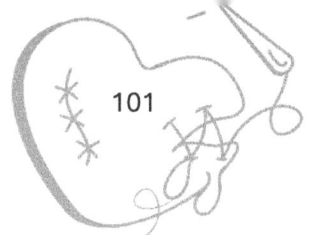

Light Through the Darkness

Even in the darkest of hours,
There's a flicker of hope that persists.
It cannot be smothered.

LIGHT THROUGH THE DARKNESS

Eternal

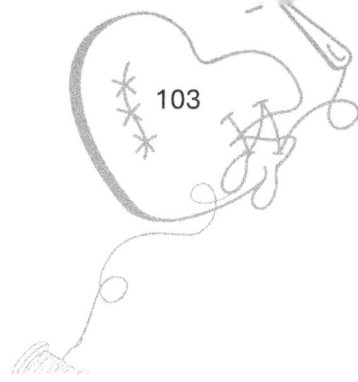

I run this race called life with every morsel of
energy I have
Not to earn a prize, but to reach my final
destination
A place where joy is forever and tears are no
more
When I've reached it, I will dance and shout and
make a beautiful noise
I will feel no more sorrow
But until then, I will enjoy the time I have left
I will reach out and embrace all I meet
I will love with an unescapable fierceness
I will teach you to be brave and bold and
believe in yourself
I will live every day with an unparalleled
enthusiasm
But there is one thing I cannot do
I can't promise to be physically with you forever
As time makes friends with no man
But this I can guarantee
That you will feel me with you always
Because although death is imminent
My light shall be eternal

Today

I am suffocating on the words I cannot say
I am drowning in this sea as it carries me away
My dreams are forever one day, one day

Wanting something for which I cannot pay
Watching the part in which I cannot play
My dreams are forever one day, one day

I want to make music but I'm afraid to play
I want to walk the path, but I don't know the way
My dreams are forever one day, one day

I look up to the sky and see the stars relay
Their message of hope trying to show me the
way
My dreams are forever one day, one day

My heart is a drum beating hard to say
"Life is a journey, and you are well on your way
Your dreams aren't forever one day, one day

Hard times will come and try to block your way
But this too shall pass, no more to stay
Your dreams aren't forever one day, one day

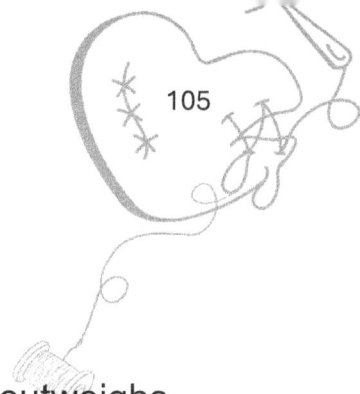

Love is the measure that overall outweighs
The troubles of life and its narrow ways
Your dreams aren't forever one day, one day

Hear these words and believe what I say
You are important and can any part play
Your dreams aren't forever one day, one day"

The words from my heart now live in my brain
I will overcome and I will find my way
My dreams aren't forever one day, one day

I'm as strong as a mountain made of stone and
clay
I will not be shaken, and my love will always
stay
My dreams start forever today, today

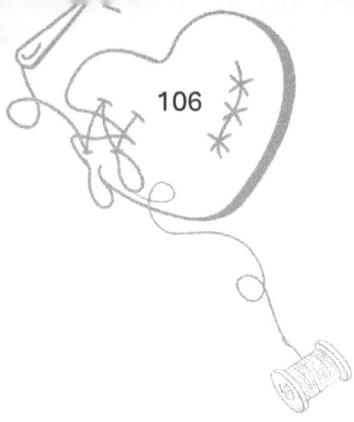

106

LIGHT THROUGH THE DARKNESS

Remember

As you journey through life's many pathways
It's extremely important to take time to pray

For it is only God who can see you through
The bumps and potholes that may be in store
for you

And when comes the time you meet a fork in
the road
He will guide you as to which way you should
go

So now as you take this path of life's newest
twists
Always remember that you are deeply missed

108

LIGHT THROUGH THE DARKNESS

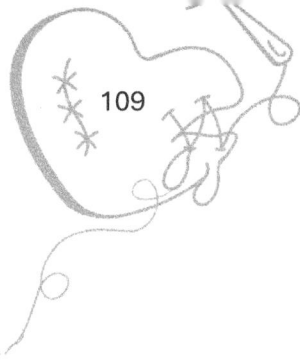

Night Skie

I cried the night I had to say goodbye
I didn't want to leave your warm embrace
I pled with God to let me stay
To let me always be able to see your face

He didn't answer how I thought that He would
He didn't give me more time to be held by you
He did however grant me my wish
He allowed me to always be in your view

Every night when the sun goes down
Don't let the sorrow steal your peace
Keep your eyes fixed on the sky above
Look very closely and you will see

I'm the biggest star shining in the night sky
Twinkling so bright and clear
God gave me the light to help brighten your
world
To remind you that I will always be here

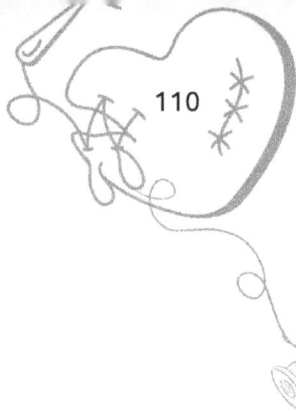

Guardian Angel

Although you cannot see me
I am living ever on
All my pain and heartache
Now and forever gone

Here up in Heaven
Is beauty beyond compare
With the crystal sea and the streets of gold
So lovely, bright, and fair

I walk daily with the Lord
Our conversation sweet
Today I posed a question
And He granted me my plea

So now whenever you feel alone
And life seems to get you down
Just listen for the wind
And focus on its sound

The wind is the sound
Of me spreading my wings
And wrapping them around you
Keeping you from harmful things

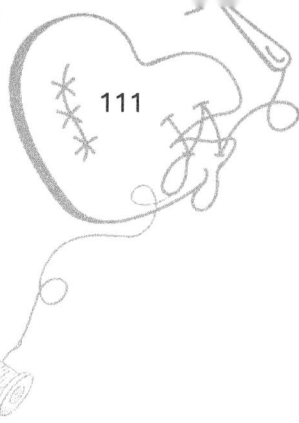

For this was the request
I asked of our God
That I could be your guardian angel
While on this earth you trod

Please don't be sad
And don't you shed a tear
For our time to be together again
Draweth ever near

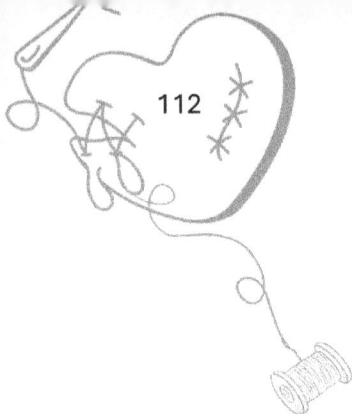

Too Weak to Fight

Lord it's me calling
I need Your help again
I am trying to fight the battle
But I am afraid I will not win

I have fought long and hard
And always did my best
To overcome every obstacle
And pass every test

With life's many trials
My faith is becoming weak
Help me to stay the course
For it is Your will that I seek

I need You to carry me
For I'm afraid I cannot walk
And please hear my heart
When I'm not strong enough to talk

You told me in Your word
That You would never leave nor forsake
So please stand by me now
Despite the wrong choices I did make

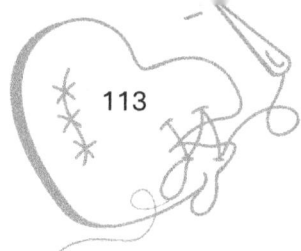

I need You to help me learn
Just which way to go
For I get confused sometimes
As You already know

I long to walk always
With You as my guide
I need You to help me
And never leave my side

So I lift to You now
All the worries in my mind
I will trust in You to lead me
Through all my troubled times

LIGHT THROUGH THE DARKNESS

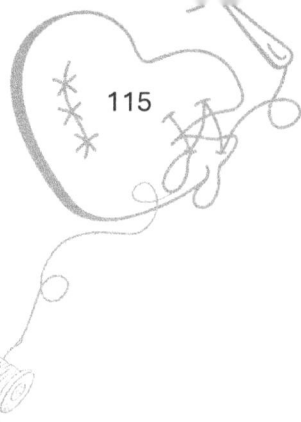

Blessed Be

When I call on Jesus
He will calm my troubled sea,
And joy comes in the morning
Is what the Bible says to me.

But life's heavy burdens
Can start to weigh me down,
It's then that my faith
Seems nowhere to be found.

And as I keep walking
Through my blackened night,
The darkness all around me
Makes it hard to see the light.

It feels as if I'm falling
Deeper and farther away,
But then I remember
He said His love will never stray.

So when my heart is heavy
And I don't know what to do,
I'll just believe in His word
And know that what He says is true.

Now when troubles get me down
And sorrow surrounds me,
I remember that God's Word told me
Blessed Be.

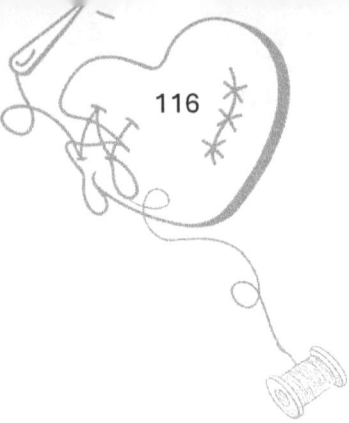

116

LIGHT THROUGH THE DARKNESS

Promises

Life
Peace
Joy
Hope
The promises I walk in

Life everlasting
Peace like a river
Joy unspeakable
Hope for tomorrow
The promises I walk in

Life everlasting, pain and sorrow no more
Peace like a river, ever flowing in my heart
Joy unspeakable, deep in my soul, springing up
Hope for tomorrow, when my tomorrow seems
bleak
The promises I walk in

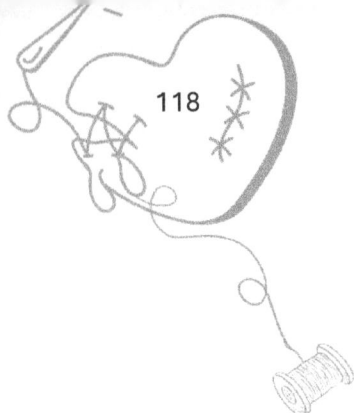

118

LIGHT THROUGH THE DARKNESS

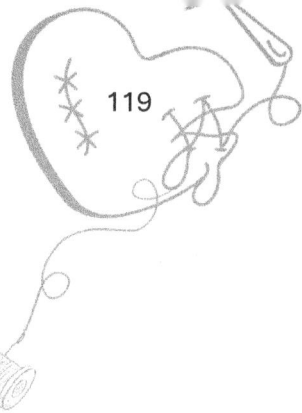

Dream or Design

My life is a dream
A series of imagined events
Some roads I've taken
Others were never meant

Some were wrong choices
A painfully destructive path
That left me battered and bruised
Still dealing with its aftermath

Some paths seemed right
A perfectly created way
With beautiful little consequences
That I will love, come what may

Some are imagined ones
A desire for something more
Though some things cannot be
No matter their allure

My life is a dream
A kaleidoscope of choices
Where some paths are nice
And others are nightmares

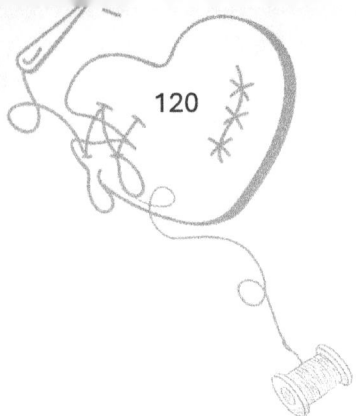

120

LIGHT THROUGH THE DARKNESS

Author's Note

If you're holding this book, I want you to know —
you are not alone.
These words came from a place of deep ache,
long nights, and honest prayers.
They're for those who cried out and heard only
silence.
For those who loved deeply, broke quietly, and
kept walking anyway.

If you didn't know how to put your pain into words
— let this be your voice.
Let this remind you that light is not the absence of
darkness,
but the refusal to let it win.

—Makenzie Rae,
with ink made of tears, writing the silent truths
that darkness tried to hide — and lighting the way
home.

AUTHOR'S NOTE

www.ingramcontent.com/pod-product-compliance
Lightning Source LLC
Chambersburg PA
CBHW032137040426
42449CB00005B/282